BRAIN BUILDER
SHAPES

BRAIN BUILDER
SHAPES

Charles Phillips

**PUZZLE
WRIGHT
PRESS**

New York

Charles Phillips would like to dedicate this book to Alison.

PUZZLE WRIGHT PRESS

New York

An Imprint of Sterling Publishing
387 Park Avenue South
New York, NY 10016

Text and puzzles copyright © 2011 by Bibelot Limited
Published by arrangement with Eddison Sadd Editions Limited, London

ISBN 978-1-4549-0031-3

Distributed in Canada by Sterling Publishing
C/o Canadian Manda Group, 165 Dufferin Street
Toronto, Ontario, Canada M6K 3H6

For information about custom editions, special sales, and premium and corporate purchases, please contact Sterling Special Sales at 800-805-5489 or specialsales@sterlingpublishing.com.

Manufactured in the United States of America

2 4 6 8 10 9 7 5 3 1

www.puzzlewright.com

CONTENTS

SECOND TEST 55

SECOND TEST ANSWERS 81

INTRODUCTION

Are you good at packing your belongings in a suitcase or fitting objects into the trunk of your car? How easy do you find it to determine whether a sofa or a table will fit through a narrow gap when you're moving to a new house or helping someone rearrange their furniture?

In many everyday situations you have to judge how shapes fit together, how lines and points in space connect. Every time you assess the angle at which you should strike a ball when you're shooting pool or playing tennis, you develop and depend upon this knowledge—without thinking about it. Likewise, when you have to determine the correct angle at which to lean a folding chair or TV tray against the wall so that it doesn't slide down, you're using the same spatial sense. Whether you're backing your car into a narrow space, stacking chairs, fitting a carpet, or designing a newsletter, you're relying on your knowledge of shapes.

How it all fits together
The study of how points, lines, 2-D shapes, and 3-D solids fit together is the basis of geometry, a field of mathematics with a vast number of practical applications in astronomy, navigation, surveying, and architecture.

Beginning as early as 3000 B.C.E., ancient peoples in the cultures of Mesopotamia, ancient Egypt, and the Indus Valley (Pakistan) proved themselves masters of this field of knowledge when building monumental tombs, temples, and altars, and in laying out their cities. Historians of mathematics report that circa 2000 B.C.E., the ancient Egyptians and the Babylonians of Mesopotamia were using their own version of the celebrated formula attributed to the ancient Greek philosopher-mathematician Pythagoras—some 1,500 years before Pythagoras's birth on the island of Samos.

● ●

The Pythagorean theorem

Think of a right-angled triangle. The theorem traditionally said to have been discovered and proven by Pythagoras states that the square of the length of the hypotenuse (the side opposite the right angle) is equal to the squares of the other two sides added together. If the hypotenuse is C and the other two sides are A and B, then $C^2 = A^2 + B^2$. (The square of a number is the total produced when a number is multiplied by itself—for example, the square of 2 is 4.)

This knowledge has many practical applications; one of its earliest was its use (in a slightly different form) by ancient Egyptians needing to create a right angle on the ground. They used a rope with twelve knotted segments and laid out a triangle with sides of three, four, and five segments: This created a right angle between the three-segment and the four-segment sides and opposite the five-segment side (the hypotenuse).

Sacred structures

Around 1800–1500 B.C.E., Aryan nomads swept into India from what is now Iran and established the Vedic culture named by scholars for the peoples' holy books, the *Vedas*. Their priests developed and used remarkably advanced geometrical expertise in building altars. They offered regular sacrifices of food and sometimes animals, and believed that pleasing the gods required all aspects of the ritual—including the precise shape and position of the altar—to be perfect. Their instructions have survived in manuals called *Sulbasutras* (800–200 B.C.E.). These include an expression of Pythagoras's theorem, values for π (that is, pi; see page 11), and instructions on how to construct a square precisely equal in area to a specific rectangle, or a circle approximately equal in area to a certain square.

- -

Practical and theoretical

While early peoples developed geometrical knowledge for its practical uses, the ancient Greeks were more interested in its theoretical applications, and formed geometry as a field of deductive reasoning, emphasizing the use of logic to prove that proposed statements about shapes and solids were true. In the fifth and fourth centuries B.C.E., the philosophers Plato and Aristotle used deductive logic to prove the truth of sets of axioms (propositions stated as truths for the purposes of argument). Then another Greek, Euclid of Alexandria, endeavored in his great work *The Elements* (circa 300 B.C.E.) to prove hundreds of geometrical theorems—all on the basis of five axioms.

Are you obtuse about angles?

Do you have bad memories of homework involving angles and triangles? Thinking about angles is essential for understanding a great range of shapes, including rectangles and squares, triangles, pentagons, hexagons—and all their many-sided cousins. This is extremely useful—and it needn't be a pain.

An angle is formed when two lines or two sections of a line cross, or when they meet at a point. If you've been camping before, for instance, think of when you're putting up a tent, and you stretch out the guy ropes from the flysheet or the tent poles to the ground. Imagine the rope to be a line running from the tent to the peg, and visualize another line running along the ground; between the two lines you will find an angle. In geometry, any shape formed by the meeting of lines will contain angles.

As you probably know, we measure angles in degrees. A full circle is 360°, a straight line is 180°, a right angle is 90°. An angle of less than 90° is called an acute angle, while one between 90° and 180° is obtuse.

Every angle between two lines is complemented by another outside the lines. Think of our guy rope connecting the tent to the ground: There is an angle between the rope and the ground, called the interior angle—in this case, it's probably about 45°; and there is a complementary one beyond the rope, up and then down to the ground, called the exterior angle. Together, the interior and the exterior angles total 180°, so if the interior angle is 45°, then the exterior angle must be 135°.

Three sides, six measurements

In a triangle—a figure with three straight sides—there are three interior angles, which total 180°. When one angle is a right angle (90°), as in the triangle described in our explanation of the Pythagorean theorem earlier, then the other two angles must total 90° between them.

In any triangle there are six key measurements: the three interior angles and the lengths of the three sides. Usually, knowing a combination of three of these measurements is enough to enable you to work out the other three. This knowledge has a host of practical applications in fields as diverse as physics, surveying, astronomy, navigation—and puzzle-solving!

Squares and more

A quadrilateral is any shape with four sides; its four interior angles total 360°. When all four sides of a quadrilateral are the same length, the shape is called a rhombus. A rectangle is a quadrilateral in which all four interior angles are right angles (each one is 90°), and a square is a rectangle that is also a rhombus. All rhombuses (as well as all rectangles) are parallelograms—four-sided shapes with two sets of sides that are parallel.

If you've ever visited the Greek capital Athens you may have climbed to the elegant hilltop temple built in honor of the goddess Athena, better known as the Parthenon. Its principal façade has a particular appeal to mathematicians because its dimensions correspond to the golden ratio, which was believed in classical times to be an expression of universal harmony and, later, in the Renaissance, to be a "divine proportion"—and which has been adopted by practitioners of architecture and fine arts over the centuries because it appears to be fine-tuned to appeal to our esthetic sense.

Imagine a line A divided into two parts: a longer part B and a shorter part C. When the ratio of the line A to the longer part B is the same as the ratio of the longer part B to the shorter part C, they are in the golden ratio. The front elevation of the Parthenon is a rectangle that can be divided into a square and a smaller rectangle: The ratio of the small rectangle to the square is the same as the ratio of the square to the larger rectangle.

The golden ratio, represented by φ (phi) is approximately 1.618034—in other words, the ratio of 1 to 1.618034 is the same as that of .618034 to 1. For more on the golden ratio and its relation to the Fibonacci sequence, check out *Brain Builder: Sequences*. (See page 13 for more about the *Brain Builder* series.)

The perfect shape?

A circle, regarded in many cultures as the perfect form, is a curved line in a flat two-dimensional surface where each point on the line is the same distance from the fixed center. A straight line from the center to any point on the circle is called the radius. A line drawn straight across from one side of the circle to the other, through the center, is called the diameter. The distance all the way around the circle is called its circumference.

As early as 2000 B.C.E., the pioneers of geometry (see page 8) knew the circumference of a circle was always a bit more than three times as long as its diameter. The ratio of the circumference to the diameter is called π (pi). One approximation of its value is $^{22}/_7$, but it's really an infinite decimal. Its digits continue to infinity without any pattern. The first six digits are 3.14159. It's been calculated (by computer, naturally) to 2.7 trillion decimal places, but even many centuries ago geometricians had produced very accurate approximations of it, from the ancient Egyptians through to the fifth-century C.E. Indian mathematician Aryabhata, who worked it out as 62,832/20,000—or 3.1416.

THINK BETTER

From humanity's earliest beginnings, people have sought to make sense of the shapes and forms around them. The great Italian physicist, philosopher, astronomer, and mathematician Galileo Galilei (1564–1642) declared that to understand the universe we need to learn the language in which it is composed, and, he went on, "it is written in mathematical language and the letters are triangles, circles, and other geometrical figures." Working with shapes is one way to hone your intelligence by considering key structures around you.

But how easy do you find it to identify and manipulate shapes? Do you sometimes wish you had a greater spatial sense—an ability to grasp structures and solids? Perhaps colleagues or family members are better than you at judging whether a picture will look good hung on a particular area of wall, or they know automatically how to stack files or pack boxes into a car most compactly, while you're still trying to figure it out. If so, don't be disheartened; there's a great deal you can do to improve your understanding of the forms that surround us all.

Seeing and making sense of shapes is a key aspect of the way we interact with our surroundings, but some of us are naturally more adept than others at shape recognition and manipulation. If you struggle with this sort of thing, it's nothing to hide or be ashamed of in any way—we all have different strengths and weaknesses, and the key to success is to identify these strong and weak points and set to work to build on our brain performance.

It's here that the puzzles in *Brain Builder: Shapes* come in. By testing and strengthening your capacity to identify and manipulate shapes, this collection of puzzles and tests will sharpen your mind, help you build your powers of spatial and numerical intelligence, and enable you to discover the elegance of geometrical logic.

USE THIS BOOK TO IMPROVE YOUR THINKING

Shapes is one of four titles in the *Brain Builder* series (see below). All four provide an enjoyable two-stage mental workout that enables you to measure your capacity for a type of thinking, then set to work at once to improve your performance as necessary.

In each book there are two series of puzzles: the First Test and the Second Test. The answer section for each test follows directly after it. As you complete the puzzles in the First Test, use the scoring system to measure your ability for that theme (see "How to score your performance" on page 14). Then, in the expanded First Test answer section, you can soak up the wealth of hints, tips, and guidance that will prepare you for the fresh challenges in the Second Test.

Take stock, then prepare to work through the Second Test, scoring your answers and comparing the totals for both tests to determine whether and how your ability for that theme has improved. Don't worry if you find your overall score hasn't increased—it's a guide only. What matters is that you start thinking about and understanding the processes involved.

Next, tackle the themes in the other three volumes of the *Brain Builder* series (*Sequences*, *Patterns*, and *Numbers*) to gain a picture of your brain's overall performance (see also the scoring chart on pages 90–91). You can then focus on the types of thinking that you need to build on first if you want to improve further. What's more, you'll soon see how this improvement can raise the quality of your thinking wherever you are and whatever you're doing—whether at work, studying, socializing, or just relaxing.

Before you start, be sure to tackle the cover puzzle (instructions are on the next page; the solution is on page 89). And remember that you'll find Notes and Scribbles pages on pages 93–95 where you can do your calculations.

The *Brain Builder* titles can help you change your habits of thinking and perception to make a real difference in your everyday life. Have fun!

COVER PUZZLE INSTRUCTIONS

To solve the cover as an interactive puzzle, make a copy and cut it into seven hexagons (as shown at right). The goal is to rearrange the hexagons to reveal the shape they conceal while creating a regular, repeating pattern in the background behind it. For a greater challenge, try solving the puzzle in your head, without cutting out the pieces.

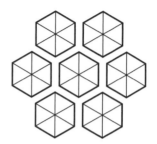

HOW TO SCORE YOUR PERFORMANCE

If you get an answer correct, award yourself 2 points. In some cases you may find that you didn't quite solve the puzzle, but you were clearly working along the right lines—in this case, award yourself 1 point. If, however, your whole approach was wrong or you couldn't see a way to answer the question at all, you score 0.

In the first answer section there's advice, background information, and Brain Builder Tips to help you improve your performance in any areas you may find difficult. In some cases, I have provided an opportunity later to have a second or even a third go at a certain type of puzzle. This gives you a chance to try out the effectiveness of the tips and advice.

BRAIN BUILDER
SHAPES

FIRST TEST

Try your hand at the twenty-five puzzles in the First Test. They are of varying degrees of difficulty—ten standard difficulty, ten medium difficulty, and five tricky. As you go, score your performance, following the guidance on page 14. Don't forget that the answer section contains advice to help you improve your performance. Good luck—and, above all, enjoy yourself!

PUZZLE 1 ON THE DANCE FLOOR

Waiting for an electrician to finish fitting a dance floor in a retro nightclub, the designer dreams up this funky grid puzzle. Each row and column in the grid contains one triangle, one square, one diamond, one circle, and two blank spaces, although not necessarily in that order. Can you complete the grid?

- Each black arrow indicates the first of the four shapes encountered when traveling in the direction of the arrow.
- Each white arrow indicates the second of the four shapes encountered in the direction of the arrow.

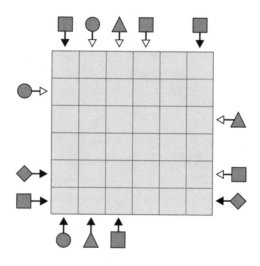

 The bottom two rows are a good place to start, especially in the lower left.

PUZZLE 2 POLYPLATES

A potter develops a range of dinner plates in the shape of triangles, rectangles, and pentagons and then devises this shape-stacker puzzle to advertise them. Can you solve it? Your task is to work out the logic behind the numbers in these shapes, and then calculate the total value of A + B.

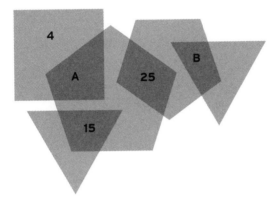

Here you need simple arithmetic and clear thinking to work out how the shapes combine, and what the numbers refer to.

Think first about which numbers might be missing.

● ●

PUZZLE 3 CUBE SEATING

After a furniture designer creates these monochrome seating blocks for a modern art gallery called "The Cube," the gallery develops this folding puzzle for its visitors. Can you solve it? The challenge is to work out which of the four cubes below is the only one that could be made using the cut-out shape.

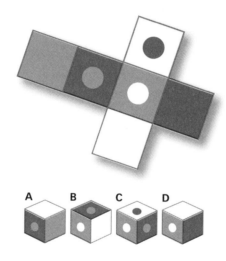

As you determine how the cut-out's six faces could be aligned in the finished cube, the puzzle develops your ability to visualize two dimensions in three.

 Merely determining whether the three given faces in each example meet at a corner won't be enough; you need to consider their orientation as well.

PUZZLE 4 SHAPE SHUFFLE

A games designer has this shape-shuffle poser created to play on the touchscreen table he keeps in his bar area at home. The task is to fill up the box so that each row, column, and long diagonal contains four different shapes and all of the letters A, B, C, and D. Each letter/shape combination may appear in the grid only once.

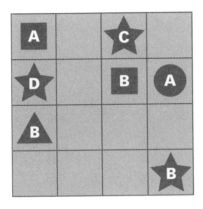

You'll find some aspects of solving this are similar to sudoku, but using simple shapes and letters in place of digits. It tests logic and your ability to visualize shape combinations in order to fill in the blank parts of the grid.

Start by solving the shapes' alignment, then move on to fitting in the letters.

PUZZLE 5 SIX SIX

A jewelry designer launches a range of hexagonal brooches, "Six Six," promoted via a monthly competition on her website. The first winner gets a complete set of the brooches. The task is to place the hexagons into the grid, without rotating any, so that where a hexagon touches another along a straight line, the contents of both adjacent triangles are the same.

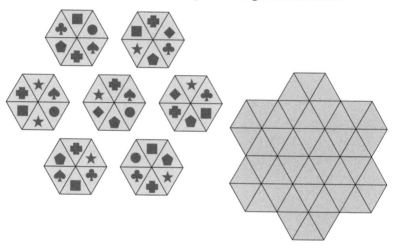

Develop your eye for visual patterning by finding the one way to fit these sets of shapes together so that they align as required. The fact that none of the hexagons rotates keeps the puzzle simple.

You can narrow down your possibilities by comparing opposite sides of different hexagons. For instance, the hexagons that have a pentagon shape on the bottom cannot be placed anywhere there would be another hexagon below them, since no hexagons have a pentagon shape at the top.

PUZZLE 6 SMOOTHIE OPERATORS

Five math teachers drink smoothies from five unusually shaped glasses while at the "GeomeTrees" vegan restaurant. They draw a grid puzzle to plot the possible combinations of teachers (1–5) and glasses (shapes). Can you solve it?

- Each row and column should contain each of the shapes and each of the numbers exactly once.
- Every square will contain one number and one shape; no combination of number and shape may be repeated anywhere in the puzzle.

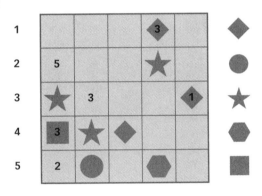

Here's a neat puzzle that provides a simple test of numerical, visual, and logical thinking all at once. It's a more complex version of Shape Shuffle (Puzzle 4).

 What shape can share the space with the 3 in the middle row?

PUZZLE 7 FINE TAILORING

A tailor loves to play around with remnants of rich velvets and silks to make fold-and-cut puzzles, and one day his boss suggests they try selling them in the local crafts shop. How's your eye for this kind of challenge? You have to determine which of the shapes—A, B, or C—is created by the series of folds and cuts shown here.

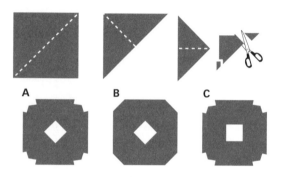

This is a version of a traditional "rainy-day activity" for children. You're required to visualize the effects of a cut when multiplied several times as the paper (or, here, the velvet) is folded out.

BRAIN BUILDER **CLUE** Can you visualize the fabric being unfolded and see in what part of the fabric the lower of the two cuts will appear?

PUZZLE 8 CARROT CAKE CUTS

One of the chefs at "GeomeTrees" (see Puzzle 6) creates this quick and easy challenge using a low-fat carrot cake she baked. The question is: Given that there are 360 degrees in a circle, how many degrees is the shaded angle?

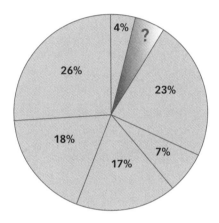

As well as engaging your visual intelligence, this puzzle presents a numerical challenge as you work out what a thin slice of the total represents in terms of degrees. Try to do it in your head.

BRAIN BUILDER CLUE   How's your arithmetic? I'm sure you can count to 100!

PUZZLE 9 CASINO SHAPES CHALLENGE

On a slow night in the casino, a dealer lays out this logical challenge for his pals.
He sets a 10-minute time limit. How quickly can you do it? The setup is this:

- Every row and column in the grid should contain one heart, one spade,
  one club, one diamond, and two blank squares, although not
  necessarily in that order.
- Every symbol with a black arrow indicates the first of the four symbols
  encountered when traveling in the direction of the arrow.
- Every symbol with a white arrow indicates the second of the four
  symbols encountered in the direction of the arrow.

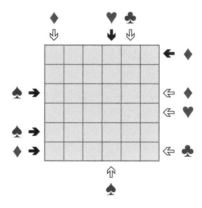

*Like Puzzle 1, this requires patience and care. Develop your visual intelligence
and positional logic as you plot the positions of the symbols in the grid.*

The diamond and spade clues on the left side the grid (and in the upper
left corner) give you a lot of information about the first column.

PUZZLE 10 WEIGHTY MATTERS

At the cooking school, a tutor surprises her students by including this challenge in the graduation exam. Each of the five different shapes represents a different weight—1, 2, 3, 4, or 5 pounds. Can you work out which shape weighs what, and how many triangles will balance the final scale?

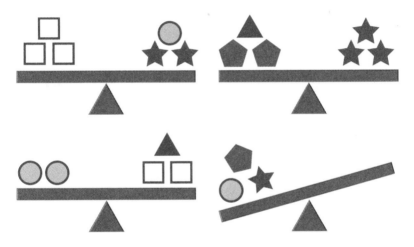

Shapes can represent quantities just as well as numbers can. The puzzle is primarily a test of numerical logic and alertness.

The scales on the left suggest that the circle represents one of the higher numbers.

PUZZLE 11 JIGSAW STAR

A new TV talent show for budding magicians uses this challenge as one of the warmups for contestants. The task is to work out which six shapes—three red and three white—can be arranged to form the star. Any may be rotated, but none may be flipped over.

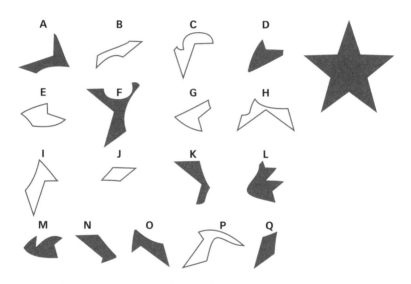

This puzzle develops your rapid-fire visual acuity as you select and combine suitable shapes.

A and F both appear to be likely candidates, but in fact only one of them is used in the jigsaw.

26

PUZZLE 12 PYRAMID PASS

In the video game "Anubis," the player is a priest in charge of mummification rites in an Ancient Egyptian temple. In this challenge a section of the temple wall becomes this symbol grid: Work out the symbol values and you may pass to the next area of the pyramid complex. Each symbol stands for a different number. In order to reach the correct total at the end of each row and column, what are the values of the circle, square, star, cross, and pentagon?

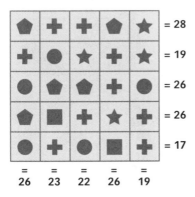

Use your facility with numbers and test your powers of deduction as you work out values for the shapes.

The second row and the middle column contain the same shapes, except for a pentagon replacing a star. You can use this information to determine the numerical difference between those two shapes. Look for other rows and columns with similar sets of shapes.

PUZZLE 13 YOGA BREAK

A yoga teacher holds a demanding position that keeps her face a few inches from the honeycomb-pattern mat for several minutes. While there, she has the idea for this jigsaw-style puzzle. The question is, which three shapes below will piece together to create the top shape?

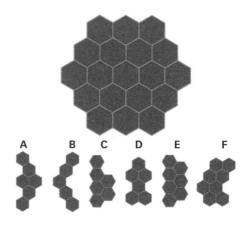

A   B   C   D   E   F

Think back to Puzzle 11. What was the best tactic for identifying compatible segments to create the larger shape? These jigsaw-style challenges are a good test of ability to visualize what shapes will look like once rotated.

When you start trying out combinations, you can eliminate some possibilities by keeping the total number of hexagons needed (19) in mind.

PUZZLE 14 SYMMETRY SLICE

Following the success of his puzzles using fabric remnants, our tailor from Puzzle 7 creates this Symmetry Slice challenge with a nice piece of tweed from one of the country suits he is making for a Scots gentleman. Your task is to cut two straight lines through this shape to create three smaller pieces that are identical to each other.

Demonstrate confidence with shapes and symmetrical lines to split this three identical ways. Try turning the book around in your hands to help you visualize what possible subsections might look like when rotated.

The two cuts needed form a continuous line, although not a straight one.

· ·

PUZZLE 15 WEDDING TILE

A lovestruck tiler decides to surprise his fiancée by creating a mosaic on her patio as a gift, completing it all in one night while she was asleep. The mosaic is made of pieces in three different shades of red, and he doesn't want any pieces of the same shade to share a border. Can you help him? The task is to plot the full mosaic, and to determine what shade pieces A and B must be in the finished design.

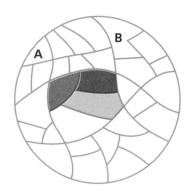

This is a mapping problem. You might refer to some of the puzzles in Brain Builder: Patterns *for comparison and inspiration. It's principally a matter of common sense and attention to detail as you plot the tiles meticulously. Using a notation system to indicate the different colors might help. Or could you solve it by doing the transformations only in your head—without making any notes on the design? That would be quite a challenge!*

Tiles that meet at a corner won't give you much information. Look at areas that are already bordered by two different colors.

PUZZLE 16 NUMBER MUGS

The shop "Numbers" sells merchandise decorated with numbers, including this range of cups and glasses. On a slow day, one rather brainy shop assistant rearranges the cups to make a number challenge for her boss. In this puzzle, the value of a shape is the number of sides the shape has multiplied by the number within it (so that a triangle containing a 4 would have a value of 12). Can you find a block of four squares—two squares wide by two squares high—with a total value of 40?

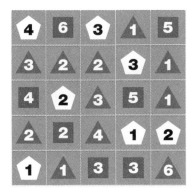

Combine visual and numerical thinking in this quick number-shape challenge.

Scan the grid for likely looking number-shape combinations. For example, any group with one or more triangles containing a low number is unlikely to be right.

PUZZLE 17 GOING PLACES

The cadets at the army training camp are given this calculation and visual-intelligence challenge as part of their graduation task. Can you solve it? Your task is to use the information provided in the grid to work out the approximate area occupied by the Jeep.

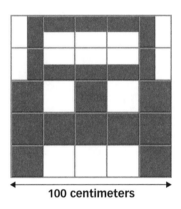

◀——————— **100 centimeters** ———————▶

Get your mental arithmetic in shape with this engaging area challenge.

  As you can see from the grid, each of the partial segments is an easily calculable part of a full square.

PUZZLE 18 KITCHEN CLUSTERS

An interior designer who's working on a mathematics professor's kitchen makes this jigsaw sudoku puzzle using refrigerator magnets. Can you help solve it? Your task is to fit the symbols shown below into the grid in such a way that each row, each column, and each of the outlined seven-square sections contains all of the symbols exactly once. Some symbols are already in place. In the refrigerator-magnet version there are enough symbol magnets to fill the whole grid, but here I have shown only one set—and left the rest to your imagination.

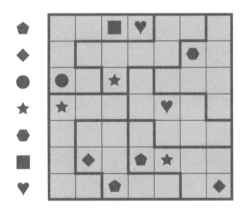

Shapes replace numbers in this intriguing sudoku variant. This will really get your visual intelligence working: Use logic to work out possible alignments.

BRAIN BUILDER **CLUE** You can often use the unusual region shapes to your advantage. For instance, note that the hexagon in the second row is in a direct line with almost all of the squares in the region to its left.

PUZZLE 19 DEADLY SHADOW

This is a puzzle taken from the Raptor Club newsletter. Only one of these shadows exactly matches that of the owl shown here as he prepares to swoop on a blithely innocent field mouse. Can you determine which outline is the owl's shadow?

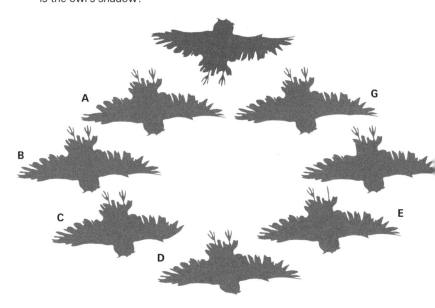

This develops your ability to work out how shapes appear when viewed from different perspectives, an important part of your visual intelligence.

You need to keep a close eye on all the details of feet, feathers, and head shape.

34

PUZZLE 20 LIKENESSES

A philosophy student starts selling pairs of "Likenesses" earrings on Etsy, where you can get a discount if you predict what one of the earrings looks like. For instance, by examining the relationship between the first pair of earring designs, can you determine which of the four shapes below (A–D) completes the same relationship in the second design?

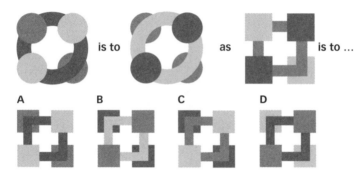

is to ... as ... is to ...

A   B   C   D

Exercise your powers of visual attention and your eye for detail by identifying sequential changes in this linked-pairs puzzle.

BRAIN BUILDER **CLUE**   Sometimes keeping track of what doesn't change helps clarify what has changed.

35

PUZZLE 21 QUEUE CUBED

In the computer shop, staff are presented with this cube-stack representation of how many people are waiting to be seen by expert technicians. When the appointments diary is full, the big cube comprises 216 small blocks—measuring 6×6×6. Small blocks disappear as people are seen. Assuming that all the blocks not visible from this angle are present, can you work out how many people have been seen—that is, how many blocks have been taken away from the cube stack?

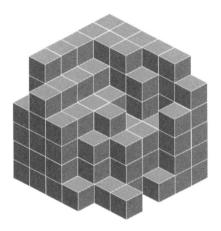

This is another puzzle that tests your basic numerical abilities alongside your facility for visualizing alignments and connections within the larger block.

Does it help to write the number of missing blocks on top of each column? Or next to each layer?

PUZZLE 22 L COMPLEMENTS O

For his friends Lewis and Oona, a puzzlemaster designs this "L complements O" anniversary card. The challenge is this: Twelve L-shapes like the ones here have been inserted in the grid and each L has one O on it. There are exactly three pieces of each of the four kinds shown here and any piece may be turned or flipped over before being put in the grid. No pieces of the same kind touch, even at a corner. Can you tell where the Ls go? One has been placed already.

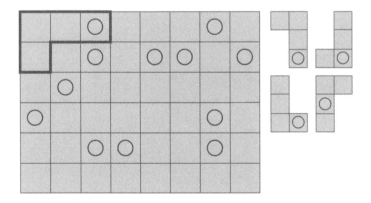

This shape-fit grid provides a great workout for your visual intelligence. You'll need to visualize a range of possible alignments as you try to determine which set is correct.

There are only two ways to legally place a piece that includes the upper right corner, and one of them leaves one of the adjacent O's stranded.

● ●

PUZZLE 23 SIMPLE SYMBOLS

A town planner commissions this symbol-placement challenge as an outdoor game for a public park. The game uses short free-standing columns with symbols on top and the player takes these to fill in a grid painted on the playground surface. Can you solve the challenge? The task is to fill in the empty squares so that each row, column, and long diagonal contains five different symbols. In the park game there are enough symbol columns to fill all the spaces, but here I am leaving it to you simply to draw in the symbols to fill the spaces in the grid.

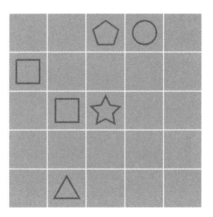

This is a more straightforward version of Puzzle 18, yet some will find it pretty challenging. Once again, it tests logic and basic visual intelligence with symbols in place of numbers on a simple grid design.

 Don't forget about the diagonals.

PUZZLE 24 SCRAMBLED

A puzzler working as a cook is inspired one morning while whisking eggs to create this puzzle. He presents it as a warmup for the weekend Recreational Mathematics conference. These pieces can be assembled to make a circle displaying a two-digit number. Can you mentally reconstruct it? (The pieces may be rotated but, unlike the eggs, not flipped over.)

Of course this puzzle would be much easier if you could physically manipulate the pieces to see how they fit together. If you find it very difficult, you could always photocopy the page, carefully cut out the pieces, then complete it as if it were a jigsaw. But the greater challenge is the original one: to perform the realignment of the pieces in your mind's eye only.

 BRAIN BUILDER CLUE   You can tell—can't you?—that one of the numbers contains a fairly long curved section.

39

. . . .

PUZZLE 25 KITES AND TRIANGLES

This puzzle is one of a popular series in the newsletter of the Kite Society. The task is simply to determine how many triangles appear in the figure.

Here's a puzzle that provides a good test of your confidence in making fine visual judgments of this kind.

 Some triangles you find will also be parts of larger triangles.

BRAIN BUILDER
SHAPES

FIRST TEST ANSWERS

Try not to turn to the answer section too quickly if you find a puzzle very hard to solve. It sometimes helps to take a break and return to it again later. When you do look up the answer, make this part of your learning—study the answer, work out the method by which it was solved, then go back to the puzzle to examine the steps taken—and determine why and how the answer is correct. This section not only provides the answers to puzzles 1–25 in the First Test (pages 15–40) but also includes hints, tips, and guidance to prepare you for puzzles 26–50 in the Second Test (pages 55–80). Do your best to absorb the extra information before you tackle the Second Test. It should help improve your brain power!

• •

Award yourself points as follows:
● Correct answer: **2 points** ● Wrong answer but on the right track: **1 point**
● Completely wrong answer or no answer at all: **0 points**

PUZZLE 1 ON THE DANCE FLOOR

The completed grid is shown below. Neither the square in the bottom row nor the diamond in the row above it can go in the first two columns.

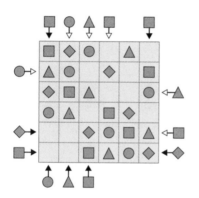

BRAIN BUILDER TIP To be good at this sort of puzzle you need strong visual logic. Practice manipulating shapes. You might try solving shape sudoku, which are just like conventional sudokus but you use a combination of shapes rather than numbers in each section of the puzzle. Puzzle 18 on page 33 is an example of this puzzle type.

PUZZLE 2 POLYPLATES

35. The numbers represent the number of sides in the shape they occupy. When shapes overlap, the numbers are multiplied. A: $4 \times 5 = 20$, B: $5 \times 3 = 15$; A + B = 20 + 15 = 35.

BRAIN BUILDER TIP With shape puzzles—and indeed any type of problem-solving—you benefit from having good powers of attention. Video games may get bad press, but research has shown that people who play action video games become practiced at paying attention to several things at once and at recovering concentration after being distracted. Perhaps you don't care for video games—in that case, how about meditation? There is now a large amount of research showing that meditation improves attention. For example, research carried out in Colorado in 2007 used volunteers performing a form of meditation in which they focused on their breathing. This showed that, over the course of a three-month retreat, their attentiveness measurably improved. Another simple technique for boosting your attention is to try to concentrate on one thing at a time—what the writer and meditation teacher Eknath Easwaran calls having "one-pointed attention."

POINTS

POINTS

PUZZLE 3 CUBE SEATING

The answer is cube **A**, as shown below. The other three options all present combinations that are physically impossible.

BRAIN BUILDER TIP When doing shape puzzles it will help you to build up your memory for images. Look out for patterns you encounter as you go about your daily business—say, tiling patterns on station walls if you are commuting. Try to commit them to memory and then test your memory later. If you're in a city, why not pop into a convenient public art gallery and do the same thing with the design of a painting. You don't have to make a beeline for the section containing abstract modern art, but this might help even more. The occipital lobes at the rear of your brain control your memory for images and are also associated with your imagination.

POINTS

PUZZLE 4 SHAPE SHUFFLE

The completed grid is shown below.

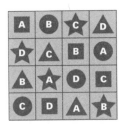

BRAIN BUILDER TIP You could practice this by making your own version of this puzzle using sixteen playing cards—say, the Jack, Queen, King, and Ace of each suit. Play around with the combinations and perhaps present it to a friend or family member as a challenge.

POINTS

PUZZLE 5 SIX SIX

The completed puzzle grid is shown below.

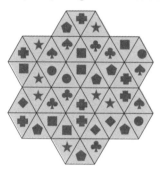

BRAIN BUILDER TIP Try the game of dominoes. It develops visual intelligence and simple logical sequencing. It's a great game to play socially, but you can also play online. And why not experiment with a colored domino set to create sequences and patterns using the dots?

POINTS

PUZZLE 6 SMOOTHIE OPERATORS

Here is the fully completed grid. As suggested by the clue, the 3 in the middle row cannot share its square with a square or diamond (which already contain a 3) or a star or circle (which appear in the same row or column), so that square contains a hexagon.

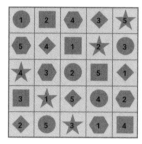

BRAIN BUILDER TIP This type of grid is called a Greco-Latin square (or an Euler square); the set of numbers or shapes alone is a Latin square. Creating your own examples is a great mental exercise, but don't try to make one that's 6×6—that's the only size of 3×3 or larger that's impossible.

POINTS

PUZZLE 7 FINE TAILORING

The answer is shape A. The lower of the two cuts creates the jagged design at the corners of the fabric.

BRAIN BUILDER TIP The best way to improve your performance at this kind of puzzle is to practice doing fold-and-cut transformations with a piece of paper and scissors; this will build your understanding of the effects of folding. Additionally, you'll benefit from trying your hand at origami, the traditional Japanese art of paper-folding. (The name comes from the Japanese words for "paper" and "fold.")

POINTS

PUZZLE 8 CARROT CAKE CUTS

The answer is 18 degrees. The percentages add up to 95 per cent, so the remaining section is 5 per cent, and 5 per cent of 360 (the total number of degrees in a circle) is 18.

BRAIN BUILDER TIP This really is a test of common sense and requires you to work out a little simple arithmetic. As I've written in other *Brain Builder* titles, it's always worth trying to build (or maintain) your facility with numbers by taking opportunities to do simple arithmetic in your head when you're shopping—or working out your share of a bill in a restaurant, say.

POINTS

45

PUZZLE 9 CASINO SHAPES CHALLENGE

The final grid is below. Here's one way to start solving this: In the first column, the diamond can't be in the top square (because it's the second shape), nor in either row in which the first shape is a spade. It can't be at the bottom (since two other shapes must fit below it). The fourth square seems like it could work, since there are two squares below it where the two other shapes could fit ... but then the bottom square would also have to be a diamond, which is impossible. So the diamond must be in the second square and the bottom square is empty. A spade must appear in the first column of one of the two rows with spade clues, otherwise there would be three empty squares in that column. That means the top and fourth squares must contain a heart and club. The fourth square can't be a heart (because of the clue on the right side of the grid), so it's a club and the heart is at the top.

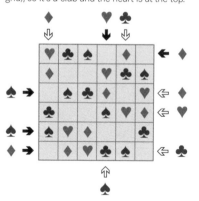

BRAIN BUILDER TIP Solving sudoku will develop some of the skills you need to tackle this challenge again (see Puzzle 42, page 72). As a general puzzling tip, you'll benefit from a positive attitude. Research shows that people who are upbeat about facing challenges do better in problem-solving and in areas such as verbal reasoning; a 1998 study found that positive moods made people more visually attentive, so their brains were more effective at seeking out information. So stay positive to improve your brain power!

POINTS

PUZZLE 10 WEIGHTY MATTERS

The pentagon weighs 1 pound, the star 2 pounds, the square 3 pounds, the triangle 4 pounds, and the circle 5 pounds. Therefore two triangles will balance the final scale.

BRAIN BUILDER TIP Practice puzzles that involve working out values for combinations of elements. You could re-create this puzzle using playing cards. Take a selection of cards—say, 10 through Ace in all four suits. Deal yourself two sets of three cards and see if you can devise values that make the two sets of cards match in total value. How long can you make it work so that the values of the cards stay constant?

POINTS

· ·

PUZZLE 11 JIGSAW STAR

A, B, E, H, K, and M complete the jigsaw as shown below.

BRAIN BUILDER TIP Do you like conventional jigsaws? Playing around with them will build the skills you need for a mental jigsaw puzzle like this. Personally, rather than clearing a table and setting out all the pieces, I prefer to play jigsaws on my smartphone. The designs are manageably small and playing them makes productive use of a few spare minutes here and there.

POINTS

PUZZLE 12 PYRAMID PASS

The different values are as follows: circle = 3, square = 7, star = 6, cross = 2, pentagon = 9. So, for example, the top row works out as 9 + 2 + 2 + 9 + 6 = 28, while the first column is 9 + 2 + 3 + 9 + 3 = 26.

BRAIN BUILDER TIP To develop your encoding skills, why not create your own shape/number code to write, say, your date of birth, or as a reminder for a number you want to keep secret (such as a banking PIN or a login for a website). You could create a shape/letter code to write your name or a secret message to a family member. For another way to recreate the puzzle for practice, take a chess set, ask a friend or family member to assign points to particular pieces, then create a layout (with the totals provided) for you to work on.

POINTS

47

PUZZLE 13 YOGA BREAK

Pieces A, C, and E combine to form the shape, as shown below. (Other rotations are possible, of course.)

BRAIN BUILDER TIP As noted in *Brain Builder: Patterns*, the ancient Chinese puzzle of tangrams develops your ability to combine shapes and see connections. When playing tangrams you build a shape using seven pieces provided in the set: You have to use all seven and none may overlap. The pieces are two large, one medium, and two small right-angled triangles; one square; and one parallelogram. Nobody knows when the puzzle was invented but it was brought back from China on trading ships to North America and Europe in the nineteenth century. You'll get a similar benefit from playing tangrams online.

POINTS

PUZZLE 14 SYMMETRY SLICE

You need to draw the two lines as shown below. The three sections created are identical and, as you can see, the dissecting "line" is continuous, though not straight.

BRAIN BUILDER TIP You can practice doing this with shapes you find in everyday life: Start with simple squares, rectangles, and so on. (Here again, a tangram set will help.) Of course, you can draw your own squares, rectangles, and triangles of various shapes on squared paper. What's the most complicated shape you can make that is divisible into three identical parts? Try one or two of your creations out on a friend or family member. As I've noted elsewhere in the *Brain Builder* series, making a puzzle enables you to come to grips with how it is put together, and this is a great help when you try to solve the same kind of puzzle again—for instance, Puzzle 44 on page 74 of this book.

POINTS

PUZZLE 15 WEDDING TILE

A must be the palest shade and **B** the darkest, as shown in the complete tiling pattern.

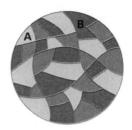

BRAIN BUILDER TIP Look at a map of your home country or area in an atlas or online and see if you can work out the smallest number of colors that could be used so that no two same colors are touching. This is a well-known problem in recreational mathematics. For a low-tech alternative, get some colored paper (say, of five different colors), cut it into random shapes and try fitting it together so that no two of the same colors touch. Then copy the design and see if you can recolor it using fewer colors.

POINTS

PUZZLE 16 NUMBER MUGS

Did you find the four shapes in the lower left part of the grid, as shown? To make 40, you combine the 4 square, the 2 pentagon, the 2 triangle, and the 2 square: $4 \times 4 = 16$, $2 \times 5 = 10$, $2 \times 3 = 6$, $2 \times 4 = 8$; $16 + 10 + 6 + 8 = 40$.

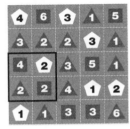

BRAIN BUILDER TIP Doing quick mental arithmetic when you get a chance will keep you primed for puzzles like this. Next time you buy a new book, see if you can work out how much the cost works out per chapter—and then per page. Or if you're traveling by train or aircraft, how much does your ticket cost per hour of journeying? Compare a night at the theater with a night at the movies—what's the comparison in terms of money units per minute?

POINTS

PUZZLE 17 GOING PLACES

The area is 6,000 cm². Each 20×20 square represents 400 cm². Ten whole squares (4,000 cm²) and ten half-squares (2,000 cm²) are used.

BRAIN BUILDER TIP This kind of puzzle helps you improve at simple geometry problems. This is another area in which a tangram set will help you. Measure the tangram pieces, make a design using some (but not all) of them, and then try to work out the area of the shape you have created. Alternatively, you could use several sets of tangrams to try to create shapes of a specific area.

POINTS

PUZZLE 18 KITCHEN CLUSTERS

The fully filled grid appears below.

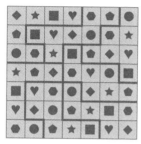

BRAIN BUILDER TIP How difficult did you find this puzzle compared to the similar challenge of Puzzle 1? Both develop your ability to visualize alignments of the shapes and require clear thinking to work out which ones must logically go where. Practicing any sudoku—whether with numbers, shapes, or other elements—will help here.

POINTS

● ●

PUZZLE 19 DEADLY SHADOW

The answer is shadow **B**. It matches exactly the outline of the owl in flight.

BRAIN BUILDER TIP To build the kind of visualization skills tested by this puzzle, try playing around with a desk lamp and using objects to create different kinds of shadows. You could start with everyday items such as a glass, a cup, a ruler, or a pair of scissors. If you have children or grandchildren, you could use some of their toys. My youngest son has recently been considering in his homework what kind of shadows are cast at different times of day and sketching the shadow of a tree with the sun in different positions. We could take a leaf out of his book. It would be interesting, say, to try sketching the shadow cast by a large square-based pyramid like those at Giza, Egypt … what would the shadow look like at dawn, 9 A.M., noon, 3 P.M., and sunset?

POINTS

PUZZLE 20 LIKENESSES

The design with the same relationship is design **D**, as shown below. The large shape swaps colors with the top-right and bottom-left shapes, and the top left shape moves behind the large shape.

BRAIN BUILDER TIP As I've suggested in other *Brain Builder* titles, your visual facility will benefit if you make an effort to be alert to designs that you encounter day to day—in newspapers, say, or on manufacturers' packaging, or in promotional material and logos. Consider whether you like the designs and why you like the ones that you do; can you come up with small improvements to ones that you like less than others? Or consider website design; imagine how the page elements might be rearranged. Exercises like this will help you stay alert to small elements in designs and layouts and this eye for detail will stand you in very good stead when addressing puzzles such as Likenesses.

POINTS

PUZZLE 21 QUEUE CUBED

The answer is 73. There are 143 small blocks remaining in the pile from the original total of 216, so 73 have been removed. One way to calculate this is to total up the blocks in each layer: 11 + 17 + 24 + 29 + 29 + 33 = 143.

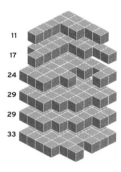

BRAIN BUILDER TIP Any puzzle that requires you to visualize three dimensions in two—or vice versa—will help build the necessary skills here. One option is to build a design like the one in the puzzle if you happen to have children's building blocks at hand. I have a large collection of small dice and can achieve the same effect with them.

POINTS

PUZZLE 22 L COMPLEMENTS O

The completed grid appears as shown below.

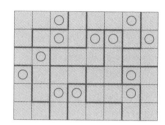

BRAIN BUILDER TIP Visit your local museum and look out for complex visual patterns on fabrics or ceramics in the collection. Repeating geometric patterns are particularly good—pay attention to how they are structured and how they repeat. Of course, you may be able to find some in your own home on old fabrics, ties, scarves, and so on. The L&O grid is another case where playing dominoes will help build the necessary visual-sequential intelligence (see also Puzzle 5).

POINTS

* *

PUZZLE 23 SIMPLE SYMBOLS

The completed grid looks as shown below, with each row, column, and long diagonal containing five different symbols.

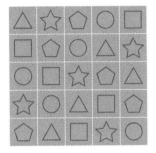

BRAIN BUILDER TIP Practicing sudoku will help with puzzles like this, especially one particular sudoku variant in which the two long diagonals also contains the digits 1 through 9 once each. You can also re-create this puzzle with playing cards (take five cards from each suit for four of the sets, and five face-down cards for the fifth set). Practicing like this should help you to discover new techniques and approaches.

POINTS

PUZZLE 24 SCRAMBLED

The number is 54, as shown below. As the Brain Builder Clue on page 39 indicated, you could tell that one of the numbers contained a curved segment and from its alignment this could not be a 2—remember that the segments are rotated and not flipped over—so it could only be a 3 or a 5.

BRAIN BUILDER TIP To help yourself do better in this type of puzzle, try making one or two number designs and cutting them up in a way that mimics the original puzzle. This will give you a sense of what sections of individual numbers look like in isolation. Keep an eye out for jigsaws containing sections with numbers in them, as these will also help.

POINTS

PUZZLE 25 KITES AND TRIANGLES

There are 35 triangles, as shown on the numbered artwork below as follows:

Single shapes: 1, 2, 3, 4, 5, 8, 9, 11. **Total 8**

Two shapes: 1/2, 1/5, 2/3, 2/6, 3/4, 3/7, 4/8, 7/8, 8/11, 10/11. **Total 10**

Three shapes: 1/2/3, 2/3/4, 2/6/9, 3/7/10, 4/8/11, 5/6/9, 6/7/8, 9/10/11. **Total 8**

Four shapes: 1/2/3/4, 2/3/6/7, 3/4/7/8, 5/6/7/8, 7/8/10/11. **Total 5**

Five shapes: 1/2/5/6/9. **Total 1**

Six shapes: 2/3/4/6/7/8, 3/4/7/8/10/11. **Total 2**

Seven shapes: 5/6/7/8/9/10/11. **Total 1**

$8 + 10 + 8 + 5 + 1 + 2 + 1 = 35$

BRAIN BUILDER TIP The single best way to improve on a particular type of puzzle is through practice. Keep an eye out online and in bookstores (or while reading newspapers) for similar challenges. Try to build your visual acuity by being alert to what you see in your day-to-day interactions. There are many opportunities to scrutinize what you view, to break images down into constituent elements, then build them back up again. Taking advantage of these opportunities will help you improve at shape puzzles such as the ones in this book.

POINTS

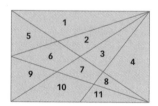

Remember the advice given earlier: Once you've completed the First Test, take a break and take stock—that way, you'll be ready to tackle the Second Test ...

BRAIN BUILDER
SHAPES

SECOND TEST

*Are you ready for the Second Test? This section offers you a
chance to try out what you've learned from the First Test and
from working through the Brain Builder Tips and background
information in the answers section to the First Test on pages
42–54. As before, there are twenty-five puzzles of varying
degrees of difficulty—ten easy, ten medium, and five tricky.
Good luck, and—once again—have fun!*

PUZZLE 26 L&O

Our puzzlemaster made a second L&O card for his friends Lewis and Oona's
joint birthday party (see Puzzle 22). As before, twelve L-shapes like the ones
here have been inserted in the grid and each L has one O on it. There are
exactly three pieces of each of the four kinds shown here and any piece may
be turned or flipped over before being put in the grid. No pieces of the same
kind touch, even at a corner. Can you tell where the L's go? One has been
placed already.

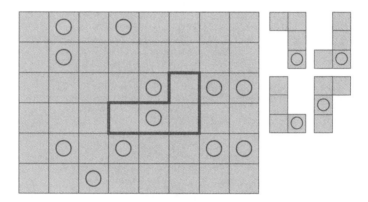

*Here's a second chance to work at this logic placement puzzle. It's only been
a few pages since we last tried it, in Puzzle 22, and it's useful to compare your
performance. This time notice any new strategies you may have adopted.*

Remember that you can eliminate any options that would place identical
L shapes next to each other.

56

PUZZLE 27 FEUDING FAMILIES

In round one of the TV game show *Feuding Families*, two families compete against one another and the clock to select which four shapes (two red and two white) can be arranged to form the pentagon shown here. Any may be rotated, but none may be flipped over. Imagine you've been drafted in at the last moment—can you help them?

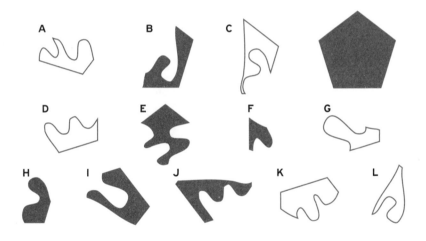

This puzzle, like Puzzle 11 in the First Test, develops your eye for detail, a key attribute for many of us performing under pressure in a demanding work environment.

BRAIN BUILDER **CLUE** You'll need some straight edges.

• •

PUZZLE 28 WARP FACTOR

An artist produces this warped rectangle for a space-age video game, "Warp Factor," where it is used as an bonus puzzle between levels. The question is, what is the sum of the internal angles of the shape?

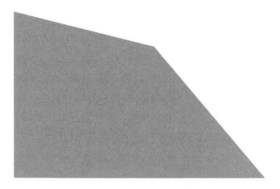

This is an intriguing new angle on a shape puzzle, and that in itself may help you find the answer.

Taking a tour of the four sides brings you all the way round to your starting point.

PUZZLE 29 TEACHERS AND TOWELS

The five teachers, on another visit to the "GeomeTrees" restaurant (see Puzzles 6 and 8) each have a different one of the five symbols below printed on their drink napkins. After a few rounds of drinks, there are enough napkins to inspire one of them to make this puzzle. Can you help the others solve it?

- Each row and column should contain each of the shapes and each of the numbers exactly once.
- Every square will contain one number and one shape; no combination of number and shape may be repeated anywhere in the puzzle.

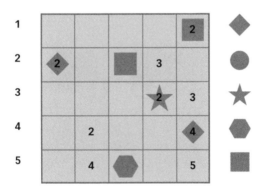

Did you find the puzzle easier to complete than before (Puzzle 6)? There have been several shape-placement puzzles calling for visual logic, so by now you're no doubt feeling sharper in this area.

BRAIN BUILDER **CLUE**   It's possible to place all the numbers before starting on the shapes.

PUZZLE 30 A SECOND LOOK AT LIKENESSES

Here is another set of "Likenesses" earrings designed by our philosophy student (see Puzzle 20). Can you solve this one? As before, your task is to determine—by examining the relationship between the first pair of earring designs—which of the four designs below has exactly the same relationship with the second design.

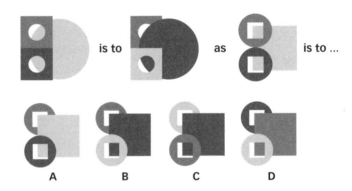

is to ... as ... is to ...

A   B   C   D

Do you feel you're making progress with this kind of challenge? Think back to Puzzle 20. You are testing and developing your powers of close attention and, in particular, your eye for detail.

Try circling any changes you notice lightly in pencil.

PUZZLE 31 THE MAGICIAN'S JACKET

Our creative tailor (see Puzzles 7 and 14) designs this patch puzzle using fabric left over from making a stage magician's jacket. By placing this patch over the grid in the right position and orientation, you can fix it so that none of the five patterns appears twice in the same row or column. The question is, where?

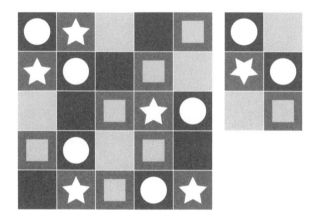

Here you develop your confidence in identifying shape patterns while using simple logic to locate the correct grid fitting.

Consider all angles, focusing your search on rows and columns that contain more than one of the same shape.

....

PUZZLE 32 CAPTAIN'S CHALLENGE

On the spaceship *Explorer*, the ship's computer creates this puzzle to test the alertness of the captain. Can you solve it? Each row and column in the grid contains one triangle, one square, one diamond, one circle, and two blank spaces, although not necessarily in that order. Can you complete the grid?

- Each black arrow indicates the first of the four shapes encountered when traveling in the direction of the arrow.
- Each white arrow indicates the second of the four shapes encountered in the direction of the arrow.

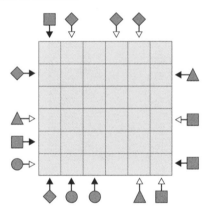

This is a second chance to try the puzzle introduced at the very start of the book (Puzzle 1). Even if you find it as challenging as before, by working at it you are developing your facility in this type of shape puzzle.

BRAIN BUILDER **CLUE** Start by trying to place the square and triangle in the first column and bottom row.

PUZZLE 33 THE GREAT DIVIDE

This is a second test of alertness and judgment set by the ship's computer aboard the spaceship *Explorer* (see Puzzle 32, opposite). Can you prove your fitness to command the ship? Your task is to divide the grid into four equally sized, equally shaped parts, each containing four gemstones of different colors.

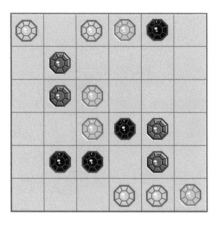

This develops your ability to identify matching sections and simple shape patterns. It's a neat test of visual intelligence.

You can draw a line between identically colored gems, because they must be in different pieces. Another general tip, if you find this challenging, is to practice cutting any 6×6 grid into four identical pieces. Start by cutting it into four 3×3 squares, and then modifying those pieces into new shapes.

PUZZLE 34 SHAPE WEIGHTS

The teacher at the cooking school (Puzzle 10) is launching a set of upmarket scales that use geometric shapes of different weights rather than traditional numbered weights. This is the puzzle she devises to run as an advertisement in the press. Can you solve it? As before, each of the five different shapes represents a different weight—1, 2, 3, 4, or 5 pounds. Your task is to work out which shape weighs what, and this time you have to determine how many stars will balance the final scale.

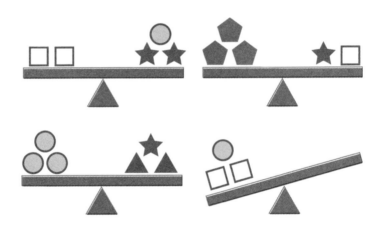

This is a test of logic and clear thinking, with a fresh angle due to its use of a shape code for the weights.

 There aren't many weight values that will work for the pentagon shape.

PUZZLE 35 BIG BIRD

The "Big Bird" poultry restaurant provides puzzles like this on its menu for the diversion of diners. Can you work out the approximate area that the bird is occupying?

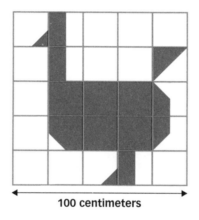

100 centimeters

As in the similar Puzzle 17, this challenge demands close attention and careful calculation. How does your solving time compare to the previous puzzle?

BRAIN BUILDER CLUE Does it make it easier if you combine partial squares?

65

PUZZLE 36 ON THE RINK

The idea for this puzzle comes to a mathematics professor while she is practicing skating in straight lines on the school's rink (certain areas of the rink are blocked off for renovation, leaving it temporarily in the shape of a pentagon). The question is, when you look at the diagram (below) of the skating moves she makes, how many triangles can you see?

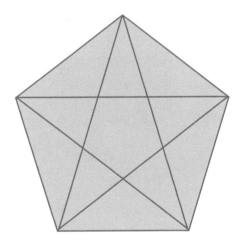

Think back to the similar Puzzle 25. This, too, is a good test of your speed of visual response. Do you notice any improvement from having done this type of puzzle before, and having thought about techniques for solving it?

You may find it helps to outline and number the triangles as you identify them. Using multiple colors may help you keep track.

PUZZLE 37 NIGHT SKY

At the observatory, a grant to fund a new telescope is celebrated with a midnight picnic and party. One of the technicians devises this puzzle for a touchscreen display. Can you solve it? The task is to determine which three of the pieces below can be used to complete the jigsaw.

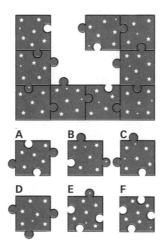

Why not set yourself a 60- or 90-second time limit for this challenge? Jigsaw-style puzzles develop your eye for shapes and their interconnections.

 BRAIN BUILDER CLUE There are only two pieces that can be used to fill the lower left of the three spaces.

- -

PUZZLE 38 SHATTERED

Exhausted at the end of his training run, an athlete flops onto the ground and imagines his numbered running vest breaking into pieces—and so he has the inspiration for this puzzle. Can you reassemble this shattered number? The pieces, when put back together, form a circle with a two-digit number on it.

Here's another puzzle in which you might benefit from setting yourself a time limit—one minute, say? Hone your mental speed and skills in recognizing shapes and identifying what may be the parts of a familiar whole.

The largest center piece gives you a very strong lead, because it can only really be part of one number.

PUZZLE 39 NUMBER PLATES

The "Numbers" shop (Puzzle 16) also sells an intriguing range of plates in geometric shapes and decorated with numbers. Our highly numerate shop assistant devises another display puzzle, this time using the plates. In this puzzle, as before, the value of a shape is the number of sides the shape has multiplied by the number within it (so a triangle containing a 4 would have a value of 12, for example). Can you find a block of four squares—two squares wide by two squares high—once again with a total value of 40?

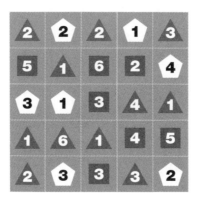

This number/shape design might make a good code, and this puzzle is a useful exercise for a codebreaker. You're developing numerical logic and rapid-fire visual intelligence.

An odd number printed on a plate with an odd number of sides will have an odd product. Since the total you're looking for is an even number, having a quick way to spot odd numbers may come in handy.

PUZZLE 40 CONFECTIONERY CUBE

The modern art gallery called "The Cube" (Puzzle 3) sells cube-shaped boxes of candy for its younger visitors. Each day a free box is offered to the first person to solve one of these cube fold-out puzzles. Would you win it? The task is to determine which one of the four options below could be made when the shape shown is folded up.

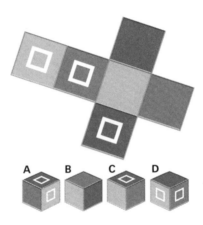

This puzzle provides a really good test of your ability to visualize shapes in three dimensions. Did you notice any benefit from having tried the task before (Puzzle 3) and from following up on the Brain Builder Tip on page 43?

Try mentally placing the indicated section of the cube on top and imagining the rest of the cube folding around it.

PUZZLE 41 SAFE SWIMMING

On a quiet day at the swimming pool, one of the lifeguards develops this shape-placement grid while doodling on his shift schedule, which shows the duties of four guards supervising four pools. Can you solve it? Fill up the box so that each row, column, and long diagonal contains four different shapes and all of the letters A, B, C, and D. Each letter/shape combination can appear in the grid only once.

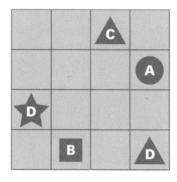

This is your second chance to have a go at this type of simple positional-logic grid, which uses shapes and letters instead of numbers. Consider your experiences solving the first time around (Puzzle 4): Did you pick up any strategies or simple insights that might help you here?

Only one shape can fit in the lower left corner, and only one letter can fit in the upper right corner.

71

PUZZLE 42 NEW DEAL AT THE CASINO

Back at the casino (Puzzle 9), our croupier with time on his hands creates another puzzle for his friends. Can you solve it? As before, the rules are:

- Every row and column in the grid should contain one heart, one spade, one club, one diamond, and two blank squares, although not necessarily in that order.
- Every symbol with a black arrow indicates the first of the four symbols encountered when traveling in the direction of the arrow.
- Every symbol with a white arrow indicates the second of the four symbols encountered in the direction of the arrow.

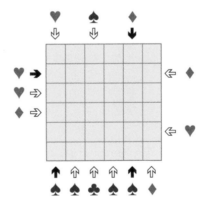

Here's a chance to further develop the positional logic you were working on when you attempted this puzzle in the First Test (Puzzle 9).

The spade clues are the key to getting started. Try to figure out the placement of the spades in the top two rows, then cross-reference with the heart clues on the left. This is a very challenging puzzle, so don't be disheartened if you find it difficult!

PUZZLE 43 A WRITER'S BLOCK

Unable to resist a superb bulk offer for printer paper, a writer buys so many boxes that his basement room is almost completely filled up with them. He stacks the boxes in a pile of 125, measuring 5×5×5. He's been using them for several months, removing them as he uses them, and now his "writer's block" appears as shown below. Assuming that all the boxes not visible from this angle are present, can you work out how many he has used?

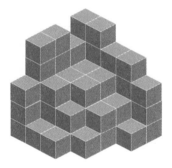

This is your second chance to try the type of challenge presented by Puzzle 21. As before, it is a good test of your ability to visualize in three dimensions.

BRAIN BUILDER CLUE If you work out how many boxes were originally in each layer, you can determine how many boxes have been taken from each before adding up these figures to get the total.

• •

PUZZLE 44 SILK SYMMETRY SLICE

This is our last visit to the garret of our creative tailor (see Puzzles 7, 14, and 31). He has made a second Symmetry Slice challenge (like Puzzle 14), this time with a piece of fine silk from a Japanese kimono he is creating. As before, your task is to cut two straight lines through the shape to create three identical pieces.

Building the skills needed to see symmetrical lines will develop your visual awareness and your ability to sketch simple designs, as well as your skill level on shape puzzles. It may help to lay a ruler (or a piece of string) across the design to try out possible divisions of the larger figure.

BRAIN BUILDER CLUE Your two cuts will be nearly parallel this time.

PUZZLE 45 DRINKS AT THE CUBE

In the bar of the modern art gallery "The Cube" (see Puzzles 3 and 40), the seats of the stools are various geometric shapes, set on a gridded floor made of cubes. One day the barman lays out the chairs in this arrangement, then sketches the layout to present it as a puzzle. The task is to fill in the empty squares so that each row, column, and long diagonal contains all five different symbols.

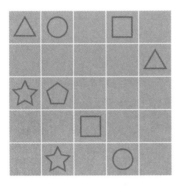

Compare your solving time to Puzzle 18 and Puzzle 23. Like those puzzles, this is a simple sudoku-like grid with shapes replacing numbers, providing a challenge for your visual awareness and clear thinking.

BRAIN BUILDER **CLUE** You might think of the diagonals as unusually shaped sudoku regions.

PUZZLE 46 SEVEN SEVEN

A retired mathematics teacher combines his love of shapes and numbers when he draws this 7×7 sudoku for his oldest friend after he realizes they have known each other for seven decades. The task is to fit the numbers 1–7 into the grid in such a way that each row, each column, and each outlined section of seven squares contains one each of all seven numbers. He's provided some numbers in place already.

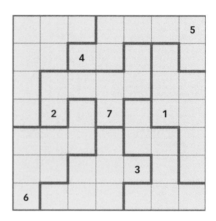

Interlocking jigsaw pieces replace more conventional blocks of squares in this neat version of a sudoku grid. It provides a test for your visual intelligence while mainly focusing on and developing numerical confidence.

You'll need some advanced solving techniques to solve this. Focusing on the middle row may help you spot some of the key steps.

PUZZLE 47 IN PROFILE

This is a test for students taking the portraiture class at an art college. Can you solve it? The task is to determine which of these shadows (A–G) is that of the young woman shown here.

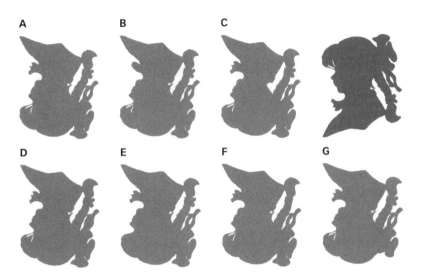

A B C

D E F G

Many of the shape puzzles in this book test and develop your attentiveness to detail; this challenge (with the associated Puzzle 19) requires the greatest focus on fine lines and minor changes.

BRAIN BUILDER **CLUE** By circling any differences you find in the shadows, you can eliminate them one by one until you isolate the one correct outline.

PUZZLE 48 ANOTHER YOGA BREAK

Our yoga teacher (Puzzle 13) devises a second jigsaw-style puzzle inspired by the pattern on her mat. As before, you have to work out which three shapes below (A–F) will fit together to create the top shape.

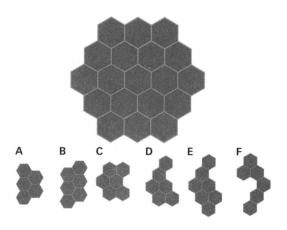

I find puzzles that require this kind of visualization quite a challenge, but I plug away at them and try to look out for similar puzzles for practice. As discussed elsewhere, we all have our strengths and weaknesses, but we can always improve if we set our minds to it.

BRAIN BUILDER CLUE Try to mentally place one of the large pieces first, since that will limit more possibilities than starting with a small one.

PUZZLE 49 GEOMETRIKEY

After many hours studying for a geometry test, a student has a dream in which the shapes below appear. She understands that she has to work out the logic behind the numbers in the shapes, and then the total of A + B. In her dream this is called a "Geomtrikey," and providing the right answer will unlock a wonderful secret.

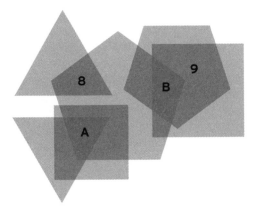

This is a matter of basic logic to unlock the key behind the numbers. Then of course you're relying on mental arithmetic to calculate the answer. And, like all the puzzles in this book, this also works at developing your confidence and skill in dealing with shapes.

 Consider simple ways in which a shape can encode a number—what can you count?

PUZZLE 50 SHAPE CONTROL

This is the third of three tests set by the ship's computer for command crew on the spaceship *Explorer* (see Puzzles 32 and 33). This time the task is to place all twelve shapes in the grid. Can you solve it, using the rules below?

- Any shape may be rotated or flipped over, but none may touch another, not even diagonally.
- The numbers outside the grid refer to the number of consecutive gray squares in each row and column, and each block is separated from the others by at least one blank square. For example, "3 2" could refer to a row with zero, one, or more blank squares, then three gray squares, then at least one blank square, then two more gray squares, followed by any number of blanks.

For this, the last puzzle in the book, I am once again combining a numerical element with a test of your ability to visualize shape combinations. Enjoy!

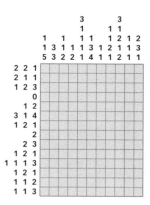

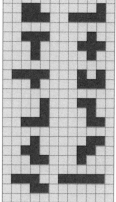

 You can tell from the number clues that the five-square block must be placed vertically.

SHAPES

SECOND TEST ANSWERS

As before, I would advise against turning to this section too hastily if you are stuck with a puzzle in the Second Test. Better to take a break, then try the puzzle again before looking up the answer. Check back to similar puzzles in the First Test and First Test Answers for clues. Then, by all means, turn to the solutions here. Don't forget to score yourself and compare your performance in the Second Test with how you did in the First Test. Then, turn to the other volumes in this series to test your thinking when it comes to puzzles involving sequences, patterns, and numbers.

Award yourself points as follows:
- Correct answer: **2 points** • Wrong answer but on the right track: **1 point**
- Completely wrong answer or no answer at all: **0 points**

PUZZLE 26 L&O

The completed grid is below. Notice that the two shapes in the lower right could be flipped together vertically, but that would place two identical shapes next to each other.

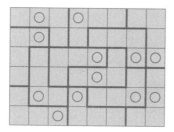

POINTS

PUZZLE 27 FEUDING FAMILIES

The pieces needed are C, D, H, and J, as shown below.

POINTS

PUZZLE 28 WARP FACTOR

The answer is 360 degrees. The internal angles of any four-sided shape total 360 degrees (see page 10, Introduction). As the Brain Builder Clue on page 58 implies, going around the four sides is equivalent—in terms of internal angles—to going round in a circle.

POINTS

PUZZLE 29 TEACHERS AND TOWELS

The completed towel arrangement in the teacher's grid should look as shown below. Because of the combination of shapes, numbers, and number-grid rules, I find this a particularly satisfying puzzle to solve.

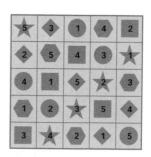

POINTS

PUZZLE 30 A SECOND LOOK AT LIKENESSES

The design with the same relationship is **B** (see below). The large shape swaps shades with the bottom-left shape, and the top-left shape goes behind the large shape.

POINTS

PUZZLE 31 THE MAGICIAN'S JACKET

You have to turn the patch on its side clockwise to fit it in along the bottom section, as shown below. This is a satisfying test of your visual intelligence.

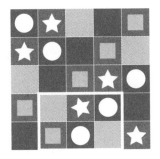

POINTS

PUZZLE 32 CAPTAIN'S CHALLENGE

The completed grid is below. In both the first column and bottom row, there is only one space in which the square and triangle can each be placed.

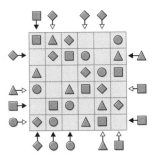

POINTS

PUZZLE 33 THE GREAT DIVIDE

The grid is shown below, with four equally sized, equally shaped parts, each containing four differently colored gems. Note that the divisions are rotationally symmetric.

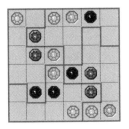

POINTS

83

PUZZLE 34 SHAPE WEIGHTS

The triangle represents 1 pound, the circle 2 pounds, the pentagon 3 pounds, the star 4 pounds, and the square 5 pounds. Therefore, three stars are needed to balance the final scale.

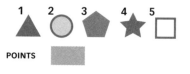

POINTS

PUZZLE 35 BIG BIRD

The answer is 3,550 cm². Each 20×20 square represents 400 cm². One way to break down the design is as shown below: five whole squares (2,000 cm²); six half-squares, one divided diagonally (1,200 cm²); one quarter-square (100 cm²), and five eighth-of-a-square triangles (250 cm²). Other approaches are possible, of course.

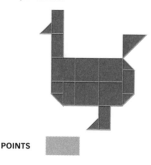

POINTS

PUZZLE 36 ON THE RINK

There are 35 triangles, shown on the numbered shape below as follows:

Single shapes: 1, 2, 3, 4, 6, 7, 8, 9, 10, 11.
    Total 10
Two shapes: 1/2, 1/4, 2/3, 3/6, 4/7, 6/11, 7/8, 8/9, 9/10, 10/11. **Total 10**
Three shapes: 1/2/3, 1/4/7, 2/5/8, 2/5/10, 3/6/11, 4/5/6, 4/5/10, 5/6/8, 7/8/9, 9/10/11.
    Total 10
Five shapes: 1/2/4/5/10, 2/3/5/6/8, 2/5/8/9/10, 4/5/6/7/8, 4/5/6/10/11. **Total 5**
10 + 10 + 10 + 5 = 35

POINTS

PUZZLE 37 NIGHT SKY

Pieces A, B, and E are needed. Only E or F could possibly fit into the lower left of the three spaces, but F proves to have the wrong kinds of connections elsewhere.

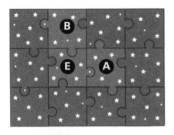

POINTS

PUZZLE 38 SHATTERED

The answer is 93, as shown. The central piece referred to in the Brain Builder clue is clearly part of a 3.

POINTS

PUZZLE 39 NUMBER PLATES

The correct section is toward the right-hand side of the bottom two rows, as shown. Combine the 1 triangle, the 4 square, the 3 square, and the 3 triangle: $(1 \times 3) + (4 \times 4) + (3 \times 4) + (3 \times 3) = 3 + 16 + 12 + 9 = 40$. There are multiple ways to quickly eliminate some areas. For example, at the far left in the second and third rows, the 5 square and the 3 pentagon together give you 35, an impossibly high number since you have to find two more shapes to total 40, and the lowest possible score for two shapes is 6 (two 1 triangles = 6).

POINTS

PUZZLE 40 CONFECTIONERY CUBE

The only cube the unfolded shape could make is cube D, as shown.

POINTS

PUZZLE 41 SAFE SWIMMING
The completed grid appears below.

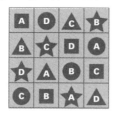

POINTS

PUZZLE 42 NEW DEAL AT THE CASINO
The grid is shown below right. The first step is to note the four spade clues below the grid. None of the spades in those columns can be in the top two rows, so the other two spades are in those rows. The spade in column 3 is second from the top, so it goes in row 2 (with a heart or diamond above), and column 6's spade is in row 1. Now look at row 3; that row's spade must be in either column 2 or 4. But note the clue indicating a heart is second from the left in that row. If there's a spade in column 2, where's the heart? Not column 1; it must go after the spade. How about column 3? Not there either, though it's trickier to see why. If there's a heart there, the square above the spade is occupied by the diamond. That leaves a club below, but the club is second from the bottom in that column, so that can't be. The heart could be in column 4, which is the trickiest to disprove. If it's there, the two squares to its right are filled with a club and diamond in that order (in the other order,

it's impossible to fill the row above without two clubs in column 6). The diamond is second from the bottom of column 6, so something is above it, which must be the club. The spade in row 4 must be in column 4 (if it were in column 1 or 5, all squares above it would have to be filled, which is not possible in those columns). In row 2, a heart is left of the spade, and the diamond and club on the right. Since the spade is second from the bottom in column 2, both squares above it are occupied; thus, the heart in row 2 is in column 2, with the square to its left empty. All column 1's empty squares are accounted for, so its heart is in row 4. Now there's nowhere for a heart in column 5. The top and bottom squares contradict the clues, and in row 5, the heart must be second from the right, but all the symbols that could go to its right are already used in that column. So the spade in row 3 must be in column 4, and the heart in column 2. (Putting the heart in column 3 leaves no space for a club in that column.) There's much more after that, but that gives you a solid start.

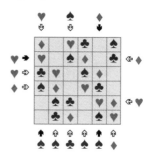

POINTS

• •

PUZZLE 43 A WRITER'S BLOCK

62. There are 63 blocks left in the pile, so 62 have been removed.

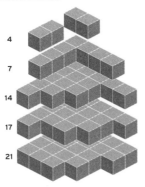

POINTS

PUZZLE 44 SILK SYMMETRY SLICE

You need to draw two lines as shown below—as you can see, they are almost parallel—to get three identical sections. I find it very satisfying when I work out the lines of symmetry in a puzzle like this. I feel as though I have uncovered another level of order beyond the one that is immediately apparent.

POINTS

PUZZLE 45 DRINKS AT THE CUBE

The completed grid looks as shown below, with each row, column, and long diagonal containing five different symbols.

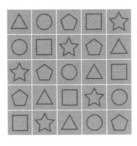

POINTS

PUZZLE 46 SEVEN SEVEN

The final grid is shown below. The clue may have helped you see that the two leftmost empty spaces in the middle row can't be a 4 or 6 and must be 3 and 5 in some order, a key deduction you'll need after some earlier steps.

3	4	2	1	7	6	5
7	6	4	3	1	5	2
1	3	6	5	4	2	7
5	2	3	7	6	1	4
2	1	7	6	5	4	3
4	5	1	2	3	7	6
6	7	5	4	2	3	1

POINTS

• •

PUZZLE 47 IN PROFILE

The answer is outline **A**, which matches the profile of the young woman's head exactly. As noted on page 34 (at the associated Puzzle 19), it's a key part of visual intelligence to be able to judge how objects will appear when seen from a different perspective. Did you find Puzzle 47 any easier having worked on Puzzle 19, and perhaps having experimented with a lamp creating shadows, as suggested in the Brain Builder Tip on page 51?

POINTS

PUZZLE 48 ANOTHER YOGA BREAK

The three pieces you need are **C**, **D**, and **E**, as shown below.

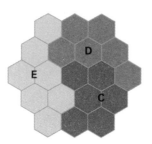

POINTS

PUZZLE 49 GEOMETRIKEY

The answer is 26. The digits represent the number of sides in the shape they occupy. When shapes overlap, the numbers are added together. A: 3 + 4 + 5 = 12, B: 4 + 5 + 5 = 14; 12 + 14 = 26.

POINTS

PUZZLE 50 SHAPE CONTROL

When all twelve pieces are in place, the grid should look as below. Did you get it right? Then you're all clear to work on the bridge of the spaceship *Explorer*!

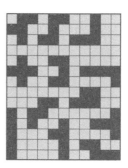

POINTS

COVER PUZZLE SOLUTION

THE BRAIN BUILDER SCORING CHART

The *Brain Builder* series comprises four volumes. In addition to *Brain Builder: Shapes*, look out for *Brain Builder: Sequences*, *Brain Builder: Patterns*, and *Brain Builder: Numbers*.

Like *Shapes*, each of the other three books also contains two sets of 25 specially themed puzzles, the First Test and the Second Test. In the First Test, you measure your capacity for the particular type of thinking covered in that book, then set about improving your performance by taking advantage of the tips and guidance provided in the First Test answers before trying the Second Test.

You can use the chart below to record your scores in the First Test and the Second Test. I've included all four books in the chart so that, as you collect the titles, you can keep track of your scores and more easily compare your performance in different types of thinking.

Book	First Test Score	Second Test Score
Shapes	....	....
Sequences	....	....
Patterns	....	....
Numbers	....	....

What your score means

For each test:

- **40 or more**—an excellent achievement.
- **35–39**—you're doing well.
- **20–34**—you have a very good basis for improving.
- **Below 20**—don't be disheartened. We all have strengths and weaknesses in particular areas, but we all also have a remarkable capacity to learn.

Don't forget, these books are designed to help you improve! The other books in the series will help you test out and build on your thinking performance in different areas. Here's what it means if you show strength in …

- *Shapes* Doing well in this volume suggests you have excellent spatial intelligence and will perform effectively when you're required to present material visually.
- *Sequences* A good score in this book indicates that you have admirable visual intelligence and are strong in logical thinking.
- *Patterns* A high score here suggests that you do well looking for connections and are good at making sense of data.
- *Numbers* A strong performance in this book suggests you are clear-thinking, accurate, and confident in situations where you have to deal quickly with numbers.

Get your brain in gear

Do you know how powerful your brain is? You have 100 billion brain cells called neurons and each one can make connections with tens of thousands of others. And not only that—every single second your brain makes a million new connections among its neurons. So there's every reason to be positive and engage your brain. Keep up the good work!

RESOURCES

Puzzle books

A History of Pi by Petr Beckmann, St Martin's Press 1976

Euclid's Window: The Story of Geometry from Parallel Lines to Hyperspace by Leonard Mlodinow, Penguin 2003

Maths Master: Making Maths Fun by Charles Phillips, Connections Book Publishing 2007 (published as *Logic Box*, Metro Books 2009, in the U.S.)

Mind's Eye Geometry: Curious and Interesting Puzzles to Amuse the Visual Imagination by Ivan Moscovich, Tarquin Publications 1994

Passage Meditation by Eknath Easwaran, Nilgiri Press 2008

Sensational Shape Problems & Other Puzzles by Ivan Moscovich, Sterling 2005

The Colossal Book of Short Puzzles and Problems by Martin Gardner, Norton 2005

The Hinged Square & Other Puzzles by Ivan Moscovich, Sterling 2005

The Math Book: From Pythagoras to the 57th Dimension, 250 Milestones in the History of Mathematics by Clifford A. Pickover, Sterling 2009

The Phantom Tollbooth by Norton Juster, HarperCollins 2008

The Thirteen Books of The Elements: Volume 1: Books 1 and 2 by Euclid, ed. Sir Thomas Heath, Dover 2000

Shapes and geometry in modern art

Abstract Art (World of Art) by Anna Moszynska, Thames & Hudson 1990

Abstract Art: The Masters of Abstraction by Dietmar Elger, Taschen 2008

Malevich (Great Modern Masters) by Jose Maria Faerna, Harry N. Abrams 1996

Painting and Understanding Abstract Art by John Lowry, The Crowood Press 2010

The 20th Century Art Book by Susannah Lawson, Phaidon Press 1996

The Shock of the New: Art and the Century of Change by Robert Hughes, Thames & Hudson 1991

Websites

www.mathsisfun.com/geometry

www.cut-the-knot.org/geometry.shtml

NOTES AND SCRIBBLES

NOTES AND SCRIBBLES

NOTES AND SCRIBBLES

ABOUT THE AUTHOR

Charles Phillips is the author of 30 books, including the best-selling *How to Think* series, and a contributor to more than 25 others, including *The Reader's Digest Compendium of Puzzles & Brain Teasers* (2001). Charles has investigated Indian theories of intelligence and consciousness in *Ancient Civilizations* (2005), probed the brain's dreaming mechanism in *My Dream Journal* (2003), and examined how we perceive and respond to color in his *Color for Life* (2004). He is also an avid collector of games and puzzles.

PUZZLE PROVIDERS
Guy Campbell; Puzzle Press